Quick Money in a Week

30 Ways to Make Money Quickly in Just One Week.

QUICK MONEY IN A WEEK

By: D.K. Hawkins
Series "Quick Money"
Version 1.1 ~November 2022
Published by D.K. Hawkins at KDP
Copyright ©2022 by D.K. Hawkins. All rights reserved.

No part of this publication may be reproduced, distributed, or transmitted in any form or by any means including photocopying, recording, or other electronic or mechanical methods or by any information storage or retrieval system without the prior written permission of the publishers, except in the case of very brief quotations embodied in critical reviews and certain other noncommercial uses permitted by copyright law.

All rights reserved, including the right of reproduction in whole or in part in any form.

All information in this book has been carefully researched and checked for factual accuracy. However, the author and publisher make no warranty, express or implied, that the information contained herein is appropriate for every individual, situation, or purpose and assume no responsibility for errors or omissions.

The reader assumes the risk and full responsibility for all actions. The author will not be held responsible for any loss or damage, whether consequential, incidental, special or otherwise, that may result from the information presented in this book.

All images are free for use or purchased from stock photo sites or royalty-free for commercial use. I have relied on my own observations as well as many different sources for this book, and I have done my best to check facts and give credit where it is due. In the event that any material is used without proper permission, please contact me so that the oversight can be corrected.

The information provided in this book is for informational purposes only and is not intended to be a source of advice or credit analysis with respect to the material presented. The information and/or documents contained in this book do not constitute legal or financial advice and should never be used without first consulting with a financial professional to determine what may be best for your individual needs.

The publisher and the author do not make any guarantee or other promise as to any results that may be obtained from using the content of this book. You should never make any investment decision without first consulting with your own financial advisor and conducting your own research and due diligence. To the maximum extent permitted by law, the publisher and the author disclaim any and all liability in the event any information, commentary, analysis, opinions, advice, and/or recommendations contained in this book prove to be inaccurate, incomplete, or unreliable or result in any investment or other losses.

Content contained or made available through this book is not intended to and does not constitute legal advice or investment advice, and no attorney-client relationship is formed. The publisher and the author are providing this book and its contents on an "as is" basis. Your use of the information in this book is at your own risk.

TABLE OF CONTENTS.

TABLE OF CONTENTS. 4

INTRODUCTION. 6

DIFFERENT WAYS TO MAKE MONEY QUICKLY IN JUST ONE WEEK. 9

   1. START AN ARTICLE DIRECTORY. 9

   2. ONLINE FOREX TRADING. 14

   3. AFFILIATE MARKETING. 19

   4. PLACING CLASSIFIED ADS ON FREE WEBSITES. 21

   5. NICHE CAMPAIGN SETUP. 27

   6. FREELANCE WRITING. 29

   7. BLOGGING. 32

   8. INTERNET MARKETING. 34

   9. VIDEO MARKETING. 37

   10. PHOTOSHOP. 41

   11. STOCK PHOTOGRAPHY. 42

   12. CRAIGSLIST. 46

   13. DELIVERY SERVICE. 49

   14. DEVELOPING A SECRET SALES FUNNEL. 50

   15. TAKING PAID SURVEYS. 54

   16. PRIVATE-LABEL PRODUCTS. 57

   17. SELLING ARTWORKS. 61

18. PODCAST. 66
19. GOOGLE ADSENSE. 71
20. PENNY STOCKS. 74
21. FORUM. 76
22. HOME-BASED DATA ENTRY JOBS. 80
23. EBOOK WRITING. 83
24. SELLING ON EBAY. 85
25. HOSTING WEBINARS. 87
26. DOMAIN FLIPPING. 90
27. PRODUCT LAUNCHING. 92
28. MEMBERSHIP WEBSITES. 93
29. TOP-TIER PROGRAMS. 96
30. ONLINE TUTORING. 99
CONCLUSION. 105

INTRODUCTION.

You can start earning money within one week. Getting your first online or offline income within a week is normal if you've opted to work online and offline and make money, whether your objective is full-time employment or just extra spending money.

Why am I saying this? Because I have witnessed it many times over the past few years as I have helped people get started making money online and offline.

Rarely do I see someone whose goal is to work online or offline and make money and who has a substantial amount of money to invest in getting started. Most would prefer to get started without substantial money or specialized skills.

This may sound like a lofty order, but happily, it can be fulfilled. It should not be surprising that making money online and offline with no cash or skills is often called "bum marketing."

You have everything you need to launch your online and offline business if you own or have access to a computer and the Internet. You lack simply clear, step-by-step directions on how to do the task. Most people will conduct an exhaustive study on making money online and offline but never start. Perhaps they simply lack confidence in their abilities.

There are so many items in the world (yes, the WORLD, not just your city, state, or country) that even with the help of a thousand of my closest friends, I could not possibly promote them all, and if you speak many languages, WOW, you have even more opportunities.

To start earning money within a week, you must get started immediately. You can't then spend a month studying, can you?

I advocate reading this book thoroughly so that you can absorb the most information in the shortest amount of time with the top 30 ways of making money quickly within a week. It also needs the least amount of effort from you.

Are you ready to get started? Kindly read on........................

DIFFERENT WAYS TO MAKE MONEY QUICKLY IN JUST ONE WEEK.

1. START AN ARTICLE DIRECTORY.

This needs a little more effort but is quite easy. What do Internet users seek? Information and plenty of it!

To launch an article directory, you need only create a basic website and request free submissions from writers. Most article writers promote something like ebooks, seminars, software, and workshops. They are always seeking free or inexpensive exposure.

Soon, you will have access to thousands more pages of content. How will you make money? Add Google ads (details below). You earn money each time someone clicks on one of your advertisements.

Many article directories accept articles on different topics, while others specialize. Only you can determine which option is best for you. I like specialty directories because, as the web grows, I believe that people will return to a directory with quality material on a single issue more often than a directory with many articles on every subject. Even when separated by category, "all-inclusive directories" are too overwhelming for me. Again, the choice is yours.

Promoting it and acquiring high-quality content for your website is key to making money with an article directory. To obtain high-quality articles on a particular topic, it is necessary to do a web search using the appropriate key terms.

Contact the author (most will have their contact information in the resource box at the end of the article) and ask them to submit articles often to your directory. They will nearly always agree.

Now is the time when your website should truly take off. Once search engines have indexed your directory, many will start sending you content automatically. Once you have a few hundred articles in your directory (and this may take as little as a few weeks if you put in the effort), slap those Google ads on each page, and voila - you have hundreds of pages of content containing advertising that, every time they're clicked, generate revenue for you.

You can automatically select content from many internet article directories to get started. When you search for "article directory," approximately 3.5 million (yes, million!) results appear.

Article Directory Software: If you are willing to spend a little money, you can acquire software that automates the entire process.

A search for "article directory software" returns nearly 500,000 results. You can purchase and install most software or have the publisher install it for you. Self-installation necessitates a high level of technical proficiency.

Before creating an article directory, I suggest devoting many hours to researching the topic through reading. Although it's a very straightforward idea, it can need much work up front, but it can pay off in spades over the months and years.

Visit Google.com to learn more about acquiring the Google advertisements that appear on many websites. Select "Marketing Programs" (a plain text button right under the search box). Click "For Web Publishers: Google AdSense" then. Click finally on "What is AdSense? Rapid tour" The application will be taught in full, and you will be able to launch it within five minutes.

If you have a passion for something and can target a highly defined niche, you can build a blog about it, add some Google AdSense advertisements and make a few hundred dollars each month without too much effort. Wish to earn more? As with anything else in life, the more time you invest, the higher your income will be.

There is even a new website, Scoopt.com, which functions as a literary agent for blogs. What am I referring to? Specifically, they "assist you in obtaining licenses for the commercial and noncommercial use of your blog." In essence, they help you sell the content of your site. View complete information on their website.

Blogs are no longer limited to venting about your most recent disastrous relationship or hair colorist's botched job. They are professional means of producing money in the present.

To read a case study demonstrating how a personal hobby may be transformed into a popular, money-making blog, visit ProBlogger.net and search "Back in Skinny Jeans." The article should be displayed. It is quite interesting to read.

To create a blog, visit blogger.com, create an account and start blogging. It's gratis!

There are no get-rich-quick scams involved. My objective at Inkwell Editing is to assist editorial and creative freelancers in earning a living wage. As many others will, I will never guarantee that you will "earn thousands a month by simply performing x." Don't trust the hype.

I've worked in the publishing industry since 1987 and as a freelancer since 1993. I've heard of and utilized many programs. The only way to earn money is to continually exert effort in some endeavor. It needs time and effort, time and effort.

The good news is that the Internet makes it easier than ever to earn a job as creative work, and it may be accomplished "quite" easily if you choose effective ways and implement them regularly.

2. ONLINE FOREX TRADING.

Has your online 4forextrading come to a halt? You enter a trade only to reverse it, resulting in a loss. Have you ever desired a method that consistently made money without requiring constant attention? I have something that you might find useful.

This section assumes you are familiar with online forex charting utilizing technical studies, including Exponential Moving Average, MACD, and Stochastics. I utilize Wizetrade Forex and MB Trading's free technical charts for my charting needs.

Initially, the disclaimer.

Foreign Exchange trading is a hard opportunity that offers above-average returns to educated and experienced traders willing to assume above-average risk. Before electing to engage in Foreign Exchange (FX) trading, you should evaluate your investment objectives, experience level, and risk tolerance.

You should never invest more money than you can afford to lose. Before adopting a new strategy on a real account, it is usually prudent to test it on paper first.

Type of strategy.

This is a longer-term plan usually takes one to two weeks to implement. It employs bar or candlestick charts with Exponential Moving Average, MACD, and Stochastics as indicators.

The Situation.

Graphs - 1 day and 1 month (either bar or candlestick) (Sometimes, a chart with a shorter time can provide clearer views. I prefer the 1 hour, 10 daylight, and the 180-minute light on Wizctrade.)

Exponential Moving Averages — (3) configurations, 4-13-50.

MACD — 5-34-7.

Probability — 13-5-5.

Entering The Industry.

Consider the MACD for confirmation of the trend's direction. After it has crossed its center line, the indicator is typically more reliable.

You want the Stochastic lines to intersect and move above the 20 for purchases and below the 80 for sales. (This is sometimes more apparent on shorter interval charts.)

Examine the moving averages now. When the 4 EMA and 13 EMA cross over the 50 EMA, in any direction, with a good movement angle and gap between the averages, it is a good moment to enter. (Declining trends for sales and rising trends for purchases.)

If the conditions mentioned above are met, consider entering the transaction.

Configuring Your Stop Loss.

Place your stop loss 30 to 50 pips below the previous day's low. This will be a wide-stop loss to eliminate you from the trade in catastrophic scenarios. I would suggest increasing your stop loss as your transaction profits. Regardless of what you do, DON'T decrease it. (If the trade were a sell, the stop loss would be above the day prior's high.)

In the Business.

Observe the trade to determine if it is approaching a resistance or support level, and keep a watch on the 4 and 13 exponential moving averages. Support and resistance may not play a significant role in this type of plan, but I would still monitor them closely.

Leaving the Market.

Watch for the 4 EMA to cross over the 13 EMA in the opposite direction of your entry after entering the trade. Check to see if your MACD has been inverted. How does your stochastic function? These are potential exit indicators. If the trend has reversed, you should cash in on your gains.

It needs the patience to develop while in the trade and know when to exit the transaction. The charts exist to assist you. Some members of our trading group have employed this method with great success.

3. AFFILIATE MARKETING.

There are countless affiliate items available for promotion. Affiliate marketing is the process of promoting a product online. Now, for novices, this may be as easy as opening a blog or Squidoo lens, both of which are rather straightforward. You then refer your visitors to your affiliate link on your website, where they make a purchase, and you are compensated.

This can be intimidating for a starter, as they must understand how to attract traffic to their site and get indexed by Google and about keywords. There are countless methods for promoting your website.

As a starter in affiliate marketing, you will initially feel overwhelmed. The steep learning curve takes months to complete. The good news is that there are programs available, some of which are free or very inexpensive, that can shorten your learning curve by weeks or months.

You must also pick what you will market; many choose for a business-in-a-box, but not everyone does. I believe that if you can find something enthusiastic about, you will be much more successful. Consider something you enjoy, then Google it with the phrase affiliate appended, and ta-da! You have options. An affiliate program exists for virtually any commodity imaginable, including ebooks, vitamins, and electronics.

The best course of action is to launch your website with your affiliate link and start your education. Thus, you can modify and apply what you learn as you progress, but you should get started first. Once one site is operational, you can go on to another.

Now, I create a new website every week on average. When I first began, it would take me a month to create a single website. So let's say one week for each site, four sites in one month, each generating passive revenue while you sleep. Iterate and repeat. I employ a one-week marketing plan, which has helped me get started.

I began this endeavor part-time five months ago with limited initial results. Since I was laid off two weeks ago, I realized I had to get serious. I spent between 10 and 12 hours every day working on this to get it operational. I was a novice and very confused. In the previous two weeks, I've made close to what I earned at my "real job," which wasn't peanuts.

The nicest part is that I enjoy it. I have compiled a guide that will shorten your learning curve and assist you in starting earning money sooner if you want to advance more quickly. The title is Affiliate Marketing Made Simple. Start making money more quickly and reduce your learning curve.

4. PLACING CLASSIFIED ADS ON FREE WEBSITES.

Since 2007, I've been fortunate to make my entire living online. Promoting affiliate items through free classified advertising on websites such as Craigslist and back page is one of my key sources of revenue.

The following are answers to four questions I am commonly asked about the back page; my preferred "go to" free classified ad site is if you want to earn money by putting advertisements on sites like this.

The advice provided here is applicable regardless of the free classified advertisements website you utilize.

Answers to Four Common Concerns Regarding the Posting of Free Ads on Backpage.

1. Which Cities to Place Ads: Backpage receives much traffic. How much? According to traffic estimate, a website that predicts the amount of traffic a website receives monthly, annually, etc., received 20,394,000 visitors in January 2013.

There are around 400 cities where you can place ads, but only a handful receive the most traffic. Listed here, depending on traffic, are the top twenty categories for placing ads on the back page to make money online quickly.

The Best Backpage Cities for Placing Free Ads.

- Miami, FL.

- Minneapolis, MN.

- New York, New York.

- Philadelphia, PA.

- Phoenix, AZ.

- San Diego, CA.

- Atlanta, GA.

- Boston, MA.

- Chicago, Illinois.

- Texas, Dallas/Fort Worth.

- Denver, CO.

- Houston, Texas.

- Las Vegas, NV.

- Los Angeles, CA.

- San Francisco, CA.

- Seattle, Washington.

- St. Louis, MO.

- Tampa, FL.

- Toronto, ON.

- Washington, District of Columbia.

Business Opportunities are one of the most popular categories for placing free advertisements. This area, "Business Offers," is where most affiliate opportunities you are likely interested in advertising will fit. "Money-making" chances are the most popular form of affiliate items to advertise to earn money quickly online.

2. Note regarding categories: Please adhere to site norms. Some marketers, for instance, promote business opportunities under the "Jobs" area. The last thing a job seeker wants is to come across an advertisement for a "pay for" business opportunity.

You pay for opportunities; you apply for jobs; be mindful of this distinction. Even if you believe you can get away with posting in the wrong category, refrain from abusing the service in this manner. It is simply unethical.

3. How Often to Place Advertisements to Make Consistent Money: At the outset of my affiliate marketing career, I posted ads daily, which I believe every newbie should do to start making consistent money (e.g., weekly, then daily).

FYI, employ other approaches, such as article marketing. Suppose affiliate marketing is something you hope to one day become a full-time career. In that case, you will likely need to combine many internet marketing strategies to earn enough to make this a reality.

4. How to Select Successful Products and/or Services
As a self-publisher, I mostly market my ebooks and a few "evergreen" affiliate products.

The most important advice I can provide for selecting profitable items is to choose those you are passionate about and/or have experience with. The rationale is that it is much easier to "believably" advocate products or services that you enjoy and/or have to experience.

There is a lot of junk on the Internet, and consumers can detect phoniness. Don't travel down that road. Affiliate marketing websites such as CommissionJunction and Clickbank offer thousands of products from which you can choose to earn money through an ad posting. Therefore, create your Internet marketing profession around reputable brands in which you have faith.

And just so you know, most affiliate programs are free to join, so there is no fee to get started.

5. NICHE CAMPAIGN SETUP.

You're an Internet marketer, but you don't have impressive results to show for it. How about I tell you what you need to start earning legitimate money online?

Spend a few minutes reading this post, and you can have a passive, profitable niche business in less than a week.

Let me start by saying that this WILL need effort; if you attempt something for the first time, it may be more difficult. The good news is that once you've set up your first campaign, subsequent efforts will be easy to manage, and if you don't neglect any processes, all your campaigns will generate passive money for years.

Here are the steps to create a profitable niche marketing campaign:

1) You must first choose a market niche in which to work. A niche is a group of individuals, including new mothers, single fathers, cat owners, newlyweds, and many others. Ensure you know the challenges individuals in that segment face and whether they are willing to spend money to address them.

2) Enroll in an autoresponder service and purchase a domain name. This will cost you little more than $30, but that is all you truly need, and you will recover those funds within a week or so.

3) Prepare your squeeze page, which has your opt-in form and offers a free guide or ebook in exchange for an email address.

4) Now, prepare the free ebook and the two ebooks you intend to sell for money. Write three 10-to-20-page guides that are brimming with useful information. Each of your guides should address a specific issue your target audience faces.

5) Compose 10 to 15 follow-up emails. The initial few emails should only contain free, valuable content; one of every four subsequent messages can be a promotional message to your subscribers. This is precisely how you will generate profits: by selling your items to individuals who trust you.

6) Write at least twenty articles that link to your squeeze page and distribute them to article directories. This will ensure that you continue to receive traffic for years to come.

Now that you've assembled it go rest or construct another one!

If you do a good job of quickly building your list, you will start earning money the next week. The best aspect is that it is entirely passive revenue!

6. FREELANCE WRITING.

Yes, internet freelance writing may be a lucrative profession. If writing is your passion and your talent, you can earn extra money online. You only need to keep in mind a few essential recommendations to identify the lucrative chances that will allow you to earn a substantial amount of money online.

If you are interested in locating these chances online, here is some advice on how to do so and how to make money from online freelance writing.

- Create website material for compensation. Content is crucial in the internet age, where practically all enterprises, companies, and even individuals desire their websites.

These website owners cannot keep up with the rate of frequently updating their sites' material. You only need to learn a few search engine optimization tactics if you have writing talent to obtain online content-writing contracts.

- Write articles. Articles are essential components of the web. In reality, as article marketing has become a cost-effective method for promoting businesses and items online, writing articles has also become a highly sought-after activity online. You can write and sell articles or discover companies or individuals online that will pay you to create articles for them.

- Explore employment markets online. Typically, these markets enable freelance writers to bid on writing tasks or offer their abilities to employers and corporations seeking quality content from freelance writers. Both sides may decide upon a price before the commencement of the assignment, and you will receive payment after completing your writing projects. You can also uncover prospects for online freelance writing by visiting online job marketplaces.

- Write ad copies. You can also write ad copy for firms if you're competent in sales language. Indeed, well-written ad copies are in demand online due to the proliferation of online advertisements and the trend of businesses moving their operations online. Take advantage of this need and earn money by creating ad copies.

- Author press releases Press release writing is an additional alternative for online freelance writers. This can also be a component of firms' and businesses' marketing efforts. Therefore, you can also get money from these writing projects.

- Write an eBook. If you have a passion for writing and another area of expertise, you can publish an eBook and sell it online. eBooks have been one of the most popular digital products sold online, and from the author's perspective, it is also one of the most profitable products you can sell online. When selling eBooks, you do not need to consider printing and publishing fees, which are among the most expensive aspects of selling your books. With eBooks, you can sell directly without worrying about distribution, as clients can always download the content online.

7. BLOGGING.

Making money with blogs is the most effective approach to begin making money online weekly. There is a great deal of ambiguity when attempting to determine the optimal strategy to monetize a blog. I felt compelled to write an essay to inform anyone seeking to establish a blog and begin earning money.

Choosing a niche for a blog is the first step toward earning money through blogging. A niche is simply a synonym for a market. Essentially, you should select a topic that you are comfortable blogging about. A topic you are enthusiastic about or at least interested in is an excellent choice.

Step two is selecting a blogging platform. A blogging platform is a software you will use to create and maintain a website blog. Excellent platforms are blogger blogs and WordPress.

I advise you to read reviews and select the finest platform for you. I recommend that you run your blog instead of using a free hosting service. Making money with blogs requires as much flexibility as possible, and having your blog provides this.

The third step is to populate your blog with sufficient content. The content of your blog is the information you present. Today, you can submit this information in textual, audio, or video format. You can do it yourself, hire a freelancer, or set up RSS feeds to feed content automatically to your blog.

The fourth step is to monetize your blog through affiliate review pages and Google Adsense advertisements. This is an excellent method for getting money with blogging. You are not even required to sell your product.

You can find many affiliate programs linked to your specialization and earn considerable income from items and residual income programs. You can integrate AdSense into your site to generate additional revenue; the best thing is that it's completely free.

Step five is to generate traffic to your blog. Free traffic methods such as search engine optimization, blog commenting, link exchange, article marketing, forum marketing, and social networking can do wonders for your website's traffic.

Once your blog receives consistent traffic and produces money, you should create a new one. Once you've completed the process for the first time, you will find that making money with blogs is rather simple.

8. INTERNET MARKETING.

Internet marketing is one of the fastest ways to earn money online. This doesn't apply to you promoting yourself but rather to your marketing for other businesses.

- You can do this if you are familiar with some Internet marketing processes. The amazing thing is that many of these ways are either free or inexpensive. For instance:

- You can create a blog for a business, contribute to it and utilize it to generate links to its website.

- You can earn them new clients by creating a social networking page for them on one or more social networking sites.

- By posting to groups and forums, you can increase the number of inbound connections to their website.

- You can perform article marketing on their behalf to drive traffic to their website.

- You can handle AdWords campaigns.

- You can write press releases to increase traffic to their website and business.

There are many ways to ensure the success of your clients. It is wonderful that these duties may be completed quickly. You can complete a substantial amount of marketing tasks in a week, allowing you to earn money quickly.

You can arrange for an upfront deposit and the balance upon completion. This puts the necessary funds in your possession immediately. To obtain the remainder, you must complete the work, so be sure to deliver results.

As you can see, Internet marketing has the potential to generate substantial revenues. You can set up a home office and do so often because people and businesses continually look for inexpensive ways to promote their businesses.

Try what I did if you need money immediately or within the hour. I am making more money today than I did in my previous business, and you can, too, if you click the link below and read the incredible true tale. I was suspicious for only ten seconds after joining before I knew what this was. You will also be beaming from ear to ear, as I was.

9. VIDEO MARKETING.

Over the past several years, much has been written on the significance of adding video marketing to your Internet marketing arsenal. This makes sense because video marketing is now effective and can be a terrific way to generate quick money every week. Let's explore the three steps that are mentioned below.

You create a promotional video for your product. You can want to market a product or service, and creating your videos is a great method. This is not as difficult as people believe. You require a low-cost video camera and microphone. You can view instructional videos on how to do this on YouTube.

Alternatively, you can use a movie-making application like Animoto. You essentially build a slide show video with images and words. This is a fantastic tool because you can add music and upload your videos directly to YouTube and other video-sharing websites.

The retailer creates the video. Many programs that you can join to earn money now feature promotional films.

The videos can be added to an existing website or blog. You can place them on a landing page, drive visitors to that page, and allow the video to promote your product or service.

This method has become prevalent in affiliate marketing and network marketing. With these business strategies, you sell products or recruit individuals to sell products on your behalf.

Your concentration is mostly on lead generation. Videos have already been produced by the firm you represent. This allows you to focus on marketing and utilizing the tools and resources they give.

Offer a video production service. If you find that you enjoy generating videos, there is a vast market for your talents that is now untapped.

You can make this as elaborate or as simple as you like. For instance, in local business marketing, you could visit a business, take photographs, sit down and write text, and then edit everything into a video that could be uploaded to the business's website.

Presently, virtually every Internet marketer could use assistance creating videos and uploading them to YouTube. Providing a video marketing service will keep you as busy as you desire and will be of great value to your clients.

These are three methods for making money through video marketing. You can be as creative as you like and earn money doing this part-time or even full-time.

It is essential to join a trend at its inception and "ride the wave." Thus, you can devise your plan of action and sales campaign and maximize your profits. You must seek out retailers that offer what you require at reasonable prices. Nothing in the world is without cost.

It can be time-consuming to search the Internet for video tutorials, but there is a shortcut. It merely needs to be located.

It is impossible to overstate videos' effect on a website. Which would you want to do: read a 300-

word text site or watch a 10-minute video demonstrating how to accomplish something step-by-step? If you're like me, the second option will apply.

You can explain anything verbally all day long, but I will get it immediately if you demonstrate it. Remember that a picture is worth a thousand words, and if that picture is animated, all the better.

Imagine discovering a resource that offers you, so to speak, a "leg up." It starts you off in sales and generates income while you are studying. That's much better! Specials and promotional websites exist; they must be discovered.

10. PHOTOSHOP.

There are simple ways to earn money quickly. You just need to know where to seek and realize that you can use your skills to make a substantial amount of money. Utilizing Photoshop is a terrific approach to earning money quickly.

This is because people are willing to pay for attractive graphics. You can make brushes, which are currently highly popular on the Internet. You can examine what is available on the Internet and compile your collection.

People will purchase them en masse. It would be best if you simply promoted yourself. There are some websites to which you can market. You could even be able to negotiate with stock photo websites.

You can also make money using Photoshop by creating your online store and selling images there. You can start your online store within a day and sell your artwork within a week. You can even enter graphic design competitions that offer lucrative prizes for the finest submissions. If you have any creativity with Photoshop, this is a terrific technique to do the task.

As you can see, it is possible to generate income from something you already possess. Images are popular on the Internet. People also need them for their blogs, websites, and print publications. They will pay for them to utilize them. They will fall in love with a fantastic image when they see it.

Try what I did if you need money immediately or within the hour. I am making more money today than I did in my previous business, and you can, too, if you click the link below and read the incredible true tale. I was suspicious for only ten seconds after joining before I knew what this was. You will also be beaming from ear to ear, as I was.

11. STOCK PHOTOGRAPHY.

Many individuals work primarily to earn money, but this may not provide them with happiness. However, some are fortunate enough to gain money by pursuing their love. One of these methods is photography. Some photographers have received professional training.

Typically, they are affiliated with an agency or work independently. But there are many more, like you and I, who simply like photographing people, objects, and events. Here is your opportunity to make money from your pastime. The universe of stock photos is yours to explore.

Before we discuss how to generate money with this hobby, let's examine what stock photography is. It is the availability of licensed pictures for certain uses. You might be surprised by the demand for stock pictures. Graphic and website designers, online advertising agencies, and publishing companies demand them.

The best thing about stock photography is that you don't need to be skilled to make money with it. All that is required is a passion for photography mixed with imagination. Gradually, you will develop the ability to advertise yourself successfully and, as a result, earn money!

Some individuals may argue that stock photography pays little for individual images. However, those who complain about this see it as a situation where "the glass is half full." True, stock photographs may be purchased for as little as $1.

However, the reality is that numerous individuals can utilize a particular picture.

Combine this with the fact that the same image can be uploaded to many websites. A quick calculation reveals that this is a surefire way to earn a handsome sum! Today, some individuals can make a living from stock photography due to its enormous earning potential.

Now, how exactly can one make money with stock photography?

Here are a few suggestions for getting started. Creating an original collection of images is the most obvious initial step. Try to integrate a sense of originality into the images and perspectives you capture.

You should consider the breadth of your intended collection. Some individuals prefer to specialize in a specific topic and become niche providers. Others want to cover a broad range of topics. Your decision is entirely up to you.

The next step in making money with stock photography is to create an online account with stock photography websites. Microstock photography firms are companies that accept images from a variety of photographers, including amateurs and hobbyists.

They have a low-price, high-volume business model. ShutterStock.com, BigStockPhoto.com, Fotolia.com, 123rf.com, and Dreamstime.com are among the most renowned microstock websites. With some of them, you can create an account.

After this, an example folder is created. This is your opportunity to demonstrate your talent and be chosen. Select some of your finest images and upload them. Here is a helpful hint. Ensure that the titles of the images you post are concise and pertinent. This can aid folks searching for images in swiftly locating relevant ones.

If you want to make money with stock photography, you should review the guidelines for each microstock site. These rules govern the kind of images that may be posted, their dimensions, technical quality, and commercial feasibility.

Aim to upload a large number of high-quality images. This will improve the likelihood that your images will be chosen and also help you achieve your goal of earning money. Continue to add additional images as time passes. You will soon realize that your hobby has become a fantastic source of income.

12. CRAIGSLIST.

If you are looking for quick cash, my first advice would be to sell on eBay. eBay has proven to be the simplest way for me to earn money online, followed by arbitrage sports betting and affiliate or network marketing. If you want to generate a substantial, sustained income that might replace your current income, affiliate or referral marketing is the way to go.

In light of the preceding, I'm going to show you a practical way to start earning money immediately in this post. College students have utilized this method to achieve weekly incomes above $300. You might earn at least $500 weekly using it if you are serious.

You will need Craigslist and an eBay account to utilize this technique fully. You will use Craigslist to obtain products at a discount to the going rate on eBay, then proceed to eBay and purchase them.

Many of the things on Craigslist's for sale section are posted by sellers in a rush to get rid of their stuff. They attempt to sell the items on eBay since they can't wait. This week, they need money for bills, rent, and food. Because they need cash immediately, many individuals are willing to sell digital cameras and other high-priced electronics for significantly less than eBay's asking price.

Electronics are secure, but you can target any category of merchandise you choose. The first step is to create an eBay account and start accumulating credits. Keep track of the going rate for products you wish to acquire.

Let's say a particular brand of digital camera sells for $200 on eBay but is advertised for $180 on Craigslist. You would contact the seller and say, "Hey, I'm willing to pay $150 for it today; let's meet at the nearby Berger King."

Over fifty percent of the time, they accept the offer. Most of these individuals are desperate for cash, so they won't mind losing twenty or thirty dollars if you offer it to them today.

Aim for three to five daily appointments. One piece of advice: be intelligent. Under no circumstances should you meet someone at their residence, enter their home or let them inside your car. Always meet in a public location, such as McDonald's, KFC, or Bergen King. This plan has existed for many years and will continue to be effective for anyone looking for simple ways to create money.

13. DELIVERY SERVICE.

Establishing a delivery service is a viable alternative that can generate income quickly. You can make this more particular, such as a laundry delivery service if you choose, or you can provide generic delivery services for everything customers need. Whether you are delivering a family supper or a new bed, there is virtually no limit to the variety of items you can provide.

It's a terrific alternative since, depending on your delivery, you can probably work it into your schedule. For example, if you transport furniture, you can schedule appointments on weekends or evenings when you are available. You only need to place a few advertisements. Even free forums, such as CraigsList.org, allow you to advertise your services for free in most locations.

You can decide only to take advantage of this chance for a few weeks if you're only seeking quick and simple ways to make money in the short term. However, it is also an excellent way to save for a vacation or holiday gifts over the long run.

Try what I did if you need money immediately or within the hour. I am making more money today than I did in my previous business, and you can too

14. DEVELOPING A SECRET SALES FUNNEL.

In this section, I will provide you with other advice on generating money online using a secret sales funnel.

Using your autoresponder series to make money online on autopilot is the first piece of advice.

Combining affiliate marketing and email marketing is the simplest approach to achieving this. Create a series of autoresponder messages for three months, six months, a year, or even two years.

Fill your autoresponder with timeless content or series. Doing so eliminates the need to update the autoresponder's text again. Make sure that the product you are promoting is also an evergreen product.

Once you have your product and email series, you can start building your mailing list. Your sales will operate automatically. Allow it to close deals and generate income for you. Certainly, this is a legitimate way to earn money online. You will generate a steady income for a very long period.

Show that you care about your readers or subscribers.

I have just demonstrated that this is the actual technique to make money online. However, you should not view your subscribers as miniature money-making machines. When people see this, they will unsubscribe from your mailing list immediately.

You must demonstrate caring for your readers or subscribers. Shower them with compassion. Let them know that you recognize their predicament. You honestly desire to assist them in resolving the issue.

When they joined your mailing list, your subscribers had certain expectations regarding the type of information they would receive. Therefore, you must keep your earlier promises to them.

Deliver the weekly newsletter if you have promised it. If you promise them a free something, you must deliver it. Unsatisfied subscribers will quit reading your emails or unsubscribe entirely.

Here is what you should emphasize in your email campaign:

Empathizing with the plight of the subscribers;

Only promote things of high quality; when conducting product reviews, you must be honest; and occasionally provide useful advice to your subscribers.

This won't generate quick cash, but it is a legitimate technique to earn money online. Doing so will undoubtedly increase trust, resulting in long-term gains.

Keep your subscribers engaged with your communications.

The ultimate goal of developing a mailing list is to establish a relationship with the subscribers before viewing this as a viable means of earning money online.

When you give a freebie as "bait" to entice a prospect to sign up for your mailing list, the subscribers will just accept the freebie and quit reading your emails.

What ought you to do? When you offer an unannounced freebie in your first email, inform your subscribers that more "surprise extras" are on the way. Then, ensure that you send out freebies approximately once each month.

This will maintain the subscribers' attention. They will open and read your email messages. You develop a relationship with your subscribers as a result. This is an excellent opportunity for you to sell them other affiliate products.

Now, do you see this legitimate online moneymaking opportunity? Simply convert a "freebie seeker" into a profitable lead.

Combining email marketing and affiliate marketing and creating other value for your subscribers by building trust and relationships is the key to making money online. Apply the advice mentioned above, and you'll have money in your bank account.

15. TAKING PAID SURVEYS.

Taking surveys is one of the easiest methods to get money online. It must be one of the simplest ways to earn other money using only a computer and internet connection, given the minimal setup time and lack of initial investment.

How to Start.

Utilize a free paid survey selection website that provides information on each survey site program in your nation. This will provide other information regarding the minimum age, the amount paid per survey, and the payment method (cash or vouchers).

Once you've identified some reputable sites that provide cash or voucher rewards, sign up for each and validate your email address. You can have discovered five or more sites on which to register, and it may take hours to complete each profile. So obtain your preferred beverage and settle in at your computer.

After enrolling, confirming, and filling out the profile, you have likely already accumulated some cash or points. These points are equivalent to the amount of cash indicated on the website. In the next few days, you should start receiving many invites via email to participate in paid surveys.

If you find one you like, clicking the link will take you to the website where the survey questionnaire is hosted. From this point on, you can have many or hundreds of questions to answer. The longer the survey, the more compensation is provided by survey sites.

In addition to cash survey invitations, you will receive invitations to cash prize draws. These should not be neglected for two reasons: a slight possibility of winning and completing them makes you a desirable candidate for future surveys.

The more surveys you complete now, the more opportunities you will have in the future and the greater your chances of winning one of those prizes, no matter how unlikely.

After completing a few cash-paying surveys on each site you choose earlier, you will have accumulated a substantial amount of cash or points. Once this hits their minimum payment barrier, you can request payment via check and occasionally PayPal. Some of them transmit payment at the end of each month automatically.

So, you've labored hard and responded to many questions regarding things you use, products you enjoy, and services you've encountered; what is your reward?

After a few weeks of typing and clicking, you might flip open an envelope with a check for anywhere between $10 and $50 or £10 and £50. If you are incredibly fortunate to be selected randomly, you could win $10,000 or £5,000 in prize money.

Taking paid surveys is the simplest way to earn money online. It is gratifying and affords you the rare opportunity to influence the world's largest corporations.

16. PRIVATE-LABEL PRODUCTS.

Private-label products are the most effective approach to making money without your product. Private label products are, in a nutshell, products that are manufactured by one business but sold under different brands.

The concept can be somewhat perplexing, so allow me to explain it. Consider that manufacturer A produces computer screens. This manufacturer will produce computer displays for anyone, but each screen must be identical.

Then, companies such as Sony or Toshiba will order products from producer A but offer them as Sony or Toshiba products. The reality is that they are the same goods, but due to branding, they may be able to charge different prices.

As long as the product is of great quality, nobody bothers if corporations engage in this practice. Sony and Toshiba don't do this for huge projects, but you can bet they do it for smaller ones. How, then, do you profit from this?

You can promote and sell your private-label products on sites like eBay. Ebooks are likely the easiest private-label products to market. Simply create a new cover and indicate that you are the author and are all set. Typically, you must purchase the rights to these ebooks, which can cost anywhere from a few dollars to many thousand dollars.

It all comes down to the quality of electronic books. It would be best if you were not as concerned about the quality because you can typically read them before you purchase them. Just be sure you have the right to sell them, or you could find yourself staring down the barrel of a lawyer's shotgun.

If you dislike selling other people's products, you can produce your own and sell private label rights. Wouldn't it be fantastic if thousands of people approached you to purchase your product? You would not receive a commission for each sale, but if you charged $100 for someone to sell your ebook and claim it as their own, it wouldn't be so awful.

Even if you wrote only one ebook per week, you would only need to sell the rights to seven or eight individuals for it to be profitable. Most individuals who purchase a book don't even read it; they just want to see dollar signs, and you should be alright with that.

However, you don't have to limit yourself to ebooks; you can create and sell different digital and physical private-label products. I only advised the digital versions because their reproduction is free. I would start selling these private-label products digitally before advancing to larger formats.

However, if you want to make money, you must start branding your products. Create a corporate name that you can stamp on all your items so that consumers will gradually associate your name with quality.

Which MP3 device would you prefer if you had a choice between an iPod and a different-colored MP3 player that did not bear the name iPod? Since individuals can only view the surface of products, they are sometimes unaware that they are identical. The only thing that matters to them is that they have an iPod and not a standard MP3 player, even though they may be identical.

When producing private label goods, branding can be a very effective tool. It doesn't matter if you want to sell them or make them because there is ample opportunity for profit. The most profitable strategy for selling private label products is to choose one and stay with it.

17. SELLING ARTWORKS.

Have you ever wondered how you can capitalize on your artistic abilities to produce other cash for your family?

My ability to "think outside the box" has been tested whenever my income has decreased, whether due to recessions, the global financial crisis, or general market fluctuations. After extensive research and trial and error, I've devised three strategies to help you make money from your work if you put them into practice.

Clever Ways To Profit From Your Art.

- Sell your artwork online and receive royalties for years to come.

- Sell your art lessons to students interested in learning "how to."

- Others sell your artwork and painting lessons.

So how is it executed?

1. Sell your artwork online and get yearly royalties.

This is my favored Smart Way No. 1 since the return is ongoing; I receive royalty checks monthly for work completed over 10 years ago. This is a very clever technique to earn money from your artwork, but you must know what you're doing to ensure success.

Who Will Pay Me For My Art?

What are Markets?

You must first determine which markets are likely to be interested in your artwork. Do you enjoy creating landscapes? Or animals? Or animated characters? Or Cars & Bikes? Or Nudes? Or are you more abstract? Or caricatures?

Each of these has distinct markets that can be utilized to generate royalties for decades. Some distributors of this type of art are jigsaw puzzle firms, computer and cell phone wallpaper providers, and homewares companies.

Each of these distinct sectors relies on creative and innovative artists like yourself to develop other "PRODUCTS" for them. Indeed, you are the product creator, while they are the product marketers. This is how it works.

2. Sell Your Art Lessons Online.

Now the obvious recommendation is to build a website and set up a shopping cart, and you'll be on your way to success, but if it were that simple, wouldn't everyone be doing it? Indeed, that isn't what you intend to do. You will distinguish yourself from the crowd and have students coming up to pay your tuition forever or as long as your art instruction remains popular.

So how will this be accomplished?

Everyone enjoys watching, correct? They love to observe others pick up suggestions on how they are doing their magic. Regardless of your inclination, if you have mastered your profession, you can generate interest in learning your techniques with this simple, cost-free methodology.

A) Create an account on YouTube.

B) Document oneself creating art.

C) Upload some introductory video lessons to YouTube.

Once you've uploaded your artwork to YouTube and all the other big video-sharing websites, monitor the traffic to your website for more information. Some of my films have received fifty thousand views in less than one year.

This is a significant amount of targeted traffic for your website, and the "Full-length films on DVD delivered to your door for $39.95" and "ebook quick download version for $29.95" offers. I have "How To. Products" that have been selling virtually daily for the past few months, and the best part is that the market is stable despite the unstable economy.

3. Have Others Sell Your Art and Art Lessons!

This is also a popular clever technique to generate money online by selling art. Creating artwork, as in Example 1, and selling tuition, as in Example 2, prepares you properly for this next step: recruiting AFFILIATES to sell your artwork on your behalf.

A vast army of people selling products online to audiences often accesses the websites they control. They spend most of their time generating content for blogs, responding to forum postings, and maintaining the website, leaving them with little time to create art like you and me.

Therefore, individuals with website traffic (many popular websites receive tens of thousands of unique visitors daily) are in a prime position to sell your merchandise, artwork on commission, and art "how to." products.

Many affiliates promoting my ebooks are only compensated IF they generate a sale. No base wage paid holidays or sick leave, and only commission on sales - that's my kind of workforce! There is nothing greater than it.

You can approach hundreds of website owners with your "this week's best-selling celebrity caricature wallpaper" and have them sell it on your behalf for a commission. There are no limitations to these rich regions, and with your wild artistic creativity, you would do well to follow these three shrewd internet strategies for profiting from your art.

18. PODCAST.

How do you wish to profit from your podcast? As a podcaster, the possibility of your podcast producing revenue is another benefit. As a podcaster, you don't have to worry about high overhead costs, and most of your podcast's earnings will be profit.

There are three primary ways to generate revenue with a podcast.

1. Generate income from commercial sponsors

Commercial podcast sponsorship is one of the most effective ways to create cash for your podcast. If you can secure a significant sponsor, your podcast can generate substantial cash. Major corporations are starting to grasp the true value of podcasting as time passes.

Paige and Gretchen, two mothers from Virginia, recognize the relevance of commercial sponsors. They host a weekly broadcast focused on mothers called MommyCast. Paige has five children, while Gretchen has two.

Earthlink and Dixie are the two major sponsors for their program. As a result, they get significant income through commercial sponsorship of their show. They likely had no idea of their podcast's popularity when they began producing it. However, Earthlink and Dixie saw the significance of their program and chose to become sponsors. http://www.mommycast.com/

If two mothers from Virginia can accomplish this, then anyone can. It makes no difference where you reside or what you podcast about. If you can attract a sizable audience, you will have a greater chance of attracting large sponsors for your podcast.

Commercial podcast sponsorship is a fantastic method to establish a substantial cash stream. If you can secure a huge sponsor, you could generate significant income as a podcaster. When two influential organizations, Earthlink and Dixie, see podcasting as a means to reach prospective customers, this is excellent news for all podcasters.

When a large sponsor advertises on traditional radio, the radio station's broadcast is wattage-restricted to a particular geographic region. With podcasting, however, there are no geographical restrictions. Anyone with a computer or MP3 player can listen to the show. Consequently, this is an outstanding selling factor for potential sponsors.

2. Generate Income through Donations.

Donations are another method to create revenue with your podcast. For instance, Adam Kempenaar and Sam Hallgren present the twice-weekly podcast Cinecast from Chicago.

They evaluate various films and provide their comments. Their podcast is quickly gaining popularity and continues to expand regularly. http://www.cinecast.com/

If you visit iTunes, you won't notice that they are highlighted in the directory of podcasts. This is a tremendous benefit for Cinecast. http://www.apple.com/itunes/podcasts/

Adam and Sam have decided to monetize their podcast by soliciting donations. On their website, there is a PayPay button that listeners can use to make a payment to their podcast. PayPal enjoys a favorable reputation and provides an ideal method for taking donations.

Presenting important information to your audience will make them appreciate your efforts and be more willing to contribute. However, Cinecast will likely be able to obtain national sponsors over time.

As your following expands, donations are a wonderful method to generate cash when you first start podcasting.

3. Profit from your website or blog.

The third method of monetizing your podcast is placing adverts on your website or blog. Google AdSense is one technique to achieve this objective. AdSense inserts advertisements on your website, and you receive compensation when a user clicks on an ad. https://www.google.com/adsense/

Using Clickbank to promote different products on your website or blog is another option to get revenue. You can market more than 10,000 ClickBank goods as an affiliate. Signing up as an affiliate with ClickBank is free, and you earn commissions whenever someone purchases a product using the links on your website. http://clickbank.com/

The key to producing cash is gaining exposure for your podcast. It would be best to inform individuals about your existence to attract a huge audience. As your audience grows over time, so will the opportunity for business sponsors. The most effective method of achieving this objective is submitting your podcast to iTunes and other podcast directories.

19. GOOGLE ADSENSE.

There are many ways to earn money with Google AdSense. The typical techniques for generating AdSense money have been tried and tested and proven quite effective. Many new publishers incorrectly believe that AdSense may only be implemented on websites and blogs. However, there are many other methods to use AdSense.

However, to function well, they often need substantial preparation and investigation and can take considerably more time to prepare and assemble. A total novice can take many months of hard work to earn money using AdSense.

However, there are other ways to earn money with Google AdSense. AdSense has expanded since its start and is now a widely utilized Pay-Per-Click system. There are currently many ways to generate money with AdSense on the web. Some of these "alternative techniques" are new and often need less time to implement and utilize.

One of the most effective methods to use AdSense is on web 2.0 sites. In a matter of days, an AdSense account can be set up on Blogger (a free blogging platform owned by Google), and if correctly designed, it can generate revenue within a few weeks.

It is incredibly simple to use and completely free to join. There are no hosting costs, domain name fees, or any other fees. Many publishers have employed bloggers to generate AdSense revenue with success.

The same is true for other Web 2.0 sites, such as HubPages, Xomba, and Squidoo. They are all free to join, and you can start earning with Google AdSense as soon as your first piece of content is published and you are accepted into the program. It is even feasible to place AdSense advertisements on your own YouTube videos.

There are now new ways to utilize adverts within AdSense that don't always need to use websites. By using AdSense for domains, for instance, you can earn money with Google.

If you have an underdeveloped domain and some empty web space, you can place a few AdSense advertisements and earn a little AdSense money from residual traffic by displaying a few AdSense ads. This only works with extremely popular domain names, but utilizing this underappreciated part of the AdSense program is possible.

There are many other ways to earn money with Google AdSense. If you are a novice, you should not only consider the usual methods of using the plan. To succeed, you must learn everything you can about its potential, and you never know; you can discover an untapped market niche that you can exploit to earn AdSense revenue.

20. PENNY STOCKS.

It has not been easy to generate money quickly with stocks; you will find that there are always obstacles in the road. The problem is typically the difficulty of locating a central location to gather accurate information on many companies with stock markets.

When compiling a list of investable equities with high value, it may appear impossible to determine where to start. However, it is a realizable objective; discover how.

Utilizing a stock picking service is one of the finest ways to earn money quickly with penny stocks.

When you find a professional stock selection service provider, they will offer you a weekly breakdown of a computer program-based database, including information on many stocks. Typically, all technical analyses must have been completed, and you will be provided with the final report.

Using a stock selection service that provides you with a complete study of potentially valuable stocks has many advantages, including the following:

- You will save the time and effort required to investigate such lucrative stocks independently.

- Since you are working with skilled stock-picking service providers, you can access many potentially profitable penny stock investments.

- You simply have a limited list of trendy penny stocks in which you can invest confidently.

- The provided analysis was created and programmed by a seasoned trader.

This is one of the finest strategies to make money quickly with stocks rather than through trial and error with every investment.

21. FORUM.

Every day, a growing number of Money Makers join the money forum. They have the foresight and recognize a potential advantage. There are many ways to earn money on a forum. Here are some effective techniques.

1) Publish quality content and grow your reputation!

Without a doubt, this is one of the top money-making tips. By enhancing your reputation, you indirectly foster friendship and confidence. Nobody entrusts their money or time to those they don't know well. Share your views in good faith.

Never make a promise you can't keep. Develop trust and friendship, and you will soon have a vast and robust network. You will soon have a team of builders working with you to generate income online as a group. Great business partners are difficult to discover, but you can anticipate many years of prosperous relationships and vast profits once you do. The limit is the sky.

2.) Use your forum signature!

Utilize short URL services such as http://be8.biz to transform your lengthy URL into a shorter version, allowing you to display more advertisements. The signature system is integrated into the forum, and you are free to use it. Most forums restrict your signature space to 150 and 250 characters, so please ensure you make the most of it.

Signatures are an effective form of marketing. Most individuals will click on a credible person's signature and will likely join the program he or she promotes. The more posts you have, the more likely moneymakers will see your signature advertisement. Upgrade your forum account to increase your exposure!

For a fair fee, you can upgrade to a paid membership on forums such as http://www.Dreamteammoney.com. Your user name will appear in a different color, and you will also receive free banner impressions. Your name will always be visible on the front, generating intrigue and increasing your exposure.

People want to know you and join the program you're joining so they can earn money with you. You'll soon realize that your messenger list is growing, and you'll meet more individuals who are also interested in making money online so that you can pursue this endeavor with your forum pals.

4.) Use forums to improve your PageRank and to be indexed quickly by the major search engines.

We are all aware that PR can boost a website's value. Most buyers favor sites with a high PR over those with a poor PR. If your website or blog receives an index or a high PR ranking from a forum, it will boost your PR ranking. On a money-related forum, I observed sites with PR 1 that received PR 2 after just one week of being indexed by SE.

If major search engines don't index your site, posting it on a forum with a high PR and traffic is one of the greatest solutions. Major search engines will soon index your site, leading to increased indirect visitors. On the Internet, traffic equals cash. Obtaining excellent visitors (Moneymakers) is essential to make money online.

5.) Leverage the expertise of other money-making geniuses! Learn from their mistakes!

Many forum users are happy to share their advice and expertise with you. For example: if a member teaches you how to save money intelligently and you save another $100 per month or $1,200 per year, you indirectly earn another $1,200 in one year, and that knowledge, which is your asset, follows you forever. Always improve your knowledge by learning from the knowledgeable. Many are willing to share their money-making strategies but are you willing to receive them?

Knowledge equals power and wealth. Always devote time to the forum to discover new techniques. Consider the money forum at your university for making money; many professors are available to serve as your mentor.

There are many other ways to earn money on forums. Remember that the sky is the limit. If you are willing to attempt new things, even the smallest ideas can earn you a fortune. Each sub-forum inside a forum has its purpose. Explore every section of the forum, and you will be astounded by what you discover.

Money making has never been made easier. Internet and technology have assisted in bringing the world closer together. Making money has always been a team effort. The world is out there for you, and so is the free forum that links you to like-minded moneymakers. It is now your turn to accept it.

22. HOME-BASED DATA ENTRY JOBS.

Home-based data entry jobs are among the most respectable and lucrative internet employment opportunities. These vocations make life easier and more comfortable for its users. These data entry jobs are the only legal and simple online opportunities available.

Every day, tens of thousands of people explore the internet for ways to earn money online and improve their level of living. Online data entry jobs are the only legitimate opportunities to earn money from home. Thus, it is simple for its customers to earn money online, as they may do it from the comfort of their homes.

These data entry jobs are completely valid and simple to perform. The only skill required to complete this job is keyboard proficiency. Anyone with a little understanding of the internet and typing may do this work and earn a substantial amount of money online.

These data entry jobs are simple; they only demand people to fill out online forms for the companies they choose to work for. The forms this program's users fill out are just ads for these companies. These companies will then compensate you in the form of commissions, which are typically substantial and paid promptly.

The number of commissions will depend on the number of sales generated by the companies as a result of your adverts appearing on various websites. There is no cap on how much you can earn with these data entry jobs, as the adverts you create are posted on multiple websites, making it easier for customers to purchase the products and increasing your commissions.

I want to continue working as a data entry clerk online indefinitely and earn a substantial income. The average commission rate for this position runs between $30 and $35 per sale. This number increases as the user's experience increases. I earn approximately $100 per week, which equates to at least $400 per month.

These occupations have many perks, including working from home and serving as one's employer.

You can take advantage of the training they provide to assist you in getting started in this profession and earning a substantial income. Utilize this opportunity and start immediately.

23. EBOOK WRITING.

One of the most effective ways to earn money from your ebooks is to provide only high-quality content. Your works must be informative, well-written, and practical for you to persuade online users to make a purchase effectively. When people realize that you provide excellent information, they are inclined to return for more and may even promote your ebooks to others.

Here are seven other fantastic ways to make money publishing eBooks:

1. Use captivating titles. Experts say that the quality of your book titles will determine 95% of your success. If they can attract attention online and thrill internet consumers, you can rest assured that your book sales will skyrocket quickly.

2. Consider profitable subjects. It will be easier to sell your ebooks if you write about incredibly engaging topics to online users. You can simply determine which topics would sell like hotcakes online by conducting keyword research and asking your potential clients what information they seek.

3. Keep your ebooks brief and straightforward. Due to their limited attention span, online consumers choose ebooks that are simple to comprehend and generally brief. Therefore, utilize basic language and explain your views and ideas in less than 30 pages.

4. Conduct research Everyone wants to obtain ebooks with comprehensive, detailed, and in-depth information to comprehend the main issue quickly. Don't forget to conduct research when creating your ebooks to gain more valuable information that might make your creations rich in substance and informative.

5. Stay away from fiction. Most Internet users won't pay money for anything that can't improve their

lives. Therefore, write about themes that might provide your readers with useful knowledge, such as step-by-step guidelines, and avoid writing about fictional subjects.

6. Fight against writer's block. This can be detrimental to your writing profession because it prevents you from being creative. The good news is that you can avoid feeling overworked by writing down all your thoughts and stepping away from your computer at least twice weekly.

7. Produce more ebooks. You'll earn more money from this activity if you can increase the number of your ebooks. You can accomplish this by increasing your writing hours or employing ghostwriters to create your material.

24. SELLING ON EBAY.

A growing number of people from all walks of life are finding that they may improve their financial situation through eBay. This section outlines five methods for generating income on eBay.

First, you might do what many others do and host an online "garage sale." You can generate revenue on eBay by selling items you no longer need. Each week, tens of thousands of people profit from this practice.

Second, you can make money on eBay by offering things to international consumers through your own eBay store.

Third, in a similar spirit, you can earn money on eBay by selling things you have made. For instance, you can sell your artistic products online if you have an artistic bent.

Fourth, many individuals are selling eBay products to generate cash for themselves and others.

Finally, when it comes to earning money on eBay, your options are essentially limitless. Your only real constraints are the extent of your imagination. eBay income has the potential to bolster your financial situation significantly.

You can lose money on much of what you do with auctions and eBay, but you can also make money; one of the most important factors is testing. If you test, you will know where to invest more and where to invest less.

25. HOSTING WEBINARS.

With so much skepticism surrounding the launch of an internet business, presenting webinars can be a wonderful method to build confidence with prospective clients because there is something wonderful about seeing the person speaking directly to you on the screen in front of you.

However, did you know that in addition to generating sales for your business (as much as 10% of webinar attendees end up purchasing), hosting a webinar can also generate demand for things you can sell? This is an excellent option if you want to establish an internet business but don't have a product to sell.

Here's how you can generate income by holding a webinar.

First, invite individuals to a free webinar.

This approach entails organizing a free webinar in which you provide a free training session on a certain subject. Then, after the webinar, you invite them to attend other webinars with you over the next seven, ten, twelve, or more weeks, during which you will walk them through the entire process step by step.

As most webinar software has recording capabilities, you can then create a whole video course that you might offer online for £100, £200, or more.

What should you include in your webinar?

Finding webinar content is easier than you would think. Here are some recommendations for your consideration.

Tell and show.

Create a PowerPoint presentation to demonstrate the functionality of your product.

Just consider.

Suppose you divide your presentation into seven sections and develop four minutes of content for each portion. In that case, you will have enough information for a 30-minute webinar before adding an introduction.

Interview a specialist.

You can also invite a specialist in your subject to answer questions during a webinar. This isn't an entirely novel notion, as this format has been utilized much before the invention of webinars, particularly in teleseminars and conference calls.

Once you have filmed your series of webinars and are ready to sell them, you can send a copy to your experts so that they can use them for free to gain further visibility.

You might take things to the next level by inviting prospective clients to your first webinar for free and charging them to attend a series of 12 subsequent webinars for a one-time investment of your choosing. £100. £200 or even £400.

This can be an effective approach to generating income from conducting webinars.

You can even get your opponents to join you by proposing a joint venture.

You can offer to advertise their webinars to your mailing list or vice versa and split the income 50/50.

It will be a question of personal preference as to which webinar software you use but hosting webinars can provide a unique opportunity to earn a substantial amount of money from the convenience of your armchair.

26. DOMAIN FLIPPING.

It has been pretty intriguing to learn that an individual might become an internet broker and start making income online. When you hear "domain flipping," you should envision purchasing domains or websites cheaply, providing minimal or no value, and selling them for a profit. This is yet another effortless method of getting money with minimal effort.

Domain flipping needs little formal education. It is a simple business that even adolescents in developing nations conduct without difficulty. If a teenager can do it, it is either enjoyable, a hobby, or a simple task.

The method will take minimal inventiveness and investment. You can acquire a creative domain name that can attract substantial traffic to a business and sell it for a high price after a period or immediately. How creative you can be in this situation will rely on your level of experience or competence in your field of work.

This is how straightforward the process may be. You only need to be near a computer and internet connection; everything else is optional. There is no excuse for being unemployed and struggling when domain flipping needs only a few hours per week.

Your level of dedication will have a significant impact on the quantity of money you will earn. If you exert greater effort, you will earn more.

27. PRODUCT LAUNCHING.

If you have a product that has to be launched, whether it's an old one you're taking over or a brand-new one, you can give it a befitting send-off by following the correct procedures. Launching a product quickly need not be challenging, but it will need a strategy.

First, you will need to consider the future. You should ensure that press releases, stories, images, etc., are written, covered, and taken months in advance. Even if you need to make minor adjustments to the information as the deadline approaches, most of the job will be completed.

It would be best if you also had a plan for ongoing promotion via blogs, forums, chat rooms, etc. Also, prepare all printed advertising and information packets two weeks in advance. A few days before your confirmed product launch, prepare a press kit and give it the last touches. Often, a rapid product launch is a question of planning.

Also, ensure that you have a backup plan for each promotion. If your product is due to make an appearance in a mall, for example, be prepared with a backup date in case it misses its cue. Sometimes these things occur without your fault. Therefore, you must be prepared.

Ensure that all media platforms are covered during the initial launch. Send pre-production news releases to all media outlets, create radio and television ads in advance, and have ready-to-go print advertisements if you want to launch a product quickly. Nothing should be left to chance.

28. MEMBERSHIP WEBSITES.

Many individuals believe that developing a membership website needs an enormous amount of effort if you create a "conventional" membership site, yes.

They should:

* A substantial commitment of time.

* Content that must be continually updated.

* Expensive and extensive scripts.

* Forum moderation.

However, if you construct a membership site with a "fixed term," you won't have these responsibilities.

All that is required is the following:

* ONE 2-5 page article is produced each week.

* An autoresponder (as you write lessons, you load them into your autoresponder, which delivers your lessons automatically to your subscribers on the days you determine)

* A system of recurrent payments (like PayPal or ClickBank)

* A predetermined duration for your membership (3, 6, 9, or 12 months)

And that concludes it!

Fixed-term membership sites are the simplest and most lucrative way to generate residual income online. Investing 2 to 5 hours per week is all it takes to get a monthly income on the Internet; it's that simple.

Here is how it operates:

A visitor to your website subscribes to your newsletter. Next, input their name and email address on a "capture page" that sends the data to your autoresponder. Then, your autoresponder emails them their lessons (usually weekly or whenever you specify).

29. TOP-TIER PROGRAMS.

Surely you've heard of the heavy hitters, individuals who make so much money online that they can hardly keep up with the influx. They are few and far between, but they all possess a secret you don't.

They are using top-tier programs to generate significant amounts of money, which they can invest in promoting lower-tier programs for future profits. This foolproof approach will ensure that your business grows twice as quickly or perhaps three times faster than those who understand how to generate income online.

What Is a Leading-Edge Program?

A premier program is a business opportunity that allows you to generate a substantial monthly income instantly. Unlike MLM opportunities, there is no requirement to recruit hundreds of individuals before you can earn money online.

These programs have a high initial cost, yet they provide excellent value. Typically, you will receive some of the best marketing tools and a personal mentor who will guide you along the path to success with their knowledge and advice. There are no other training programs that provide superior instruction.

The Program's Functionality.

Premium programs have a high entry fee. This may discourage those not committed to succeeding in their desire to make money online, which may be another reason these programs have a high success rate.

In most programs, only roughly 3% of people make money online, while 97% fail. However, with a top-tier program, the figures are inverted, with 97% of people succeeding and generating money and only 3% failing.

It just takes a few sales to recoup the initial investment; after that, everything is profit. Top-tier systems are easily reproducible, and virtually anyone can learn how to make the system function in a matter of days, thanks to their effective marketing and instructional strategies. There is no faster or simpler method.

Who Must Select One?

If interested, you will be required to make a sizeable initial commitment. A decent starting point is $2,000 to $4,000 to ensure you have enough to purchase into the program and spend on the first promotion to generate the initial sales required to keep the machine running. In addition to the initial cost, time will also be required.

Typically, four 4-hour days are required for training, learning, and setting up. After that, you will have to be able to devote time. The minimum requirement is 1-2 hours daily, four days weekly.

You must add more if you truly want to speed up the process. In addition to a telephone and internet connection, you must have an unlimited long-distance plan, as you will be making many calls. Meet these prerequisites, and you will quickly earn money online.

The Benefits You Will Enjoy.

If you meet the qualifications and believe a program like this suits you, you will be rewarded handsomely. When you've perfected the system, you'll have significantly more free time and likely earn twice as much money for half the amount of effort.

Even a modest investment in a top-tier program will generate a five-figure monthly income starting in the first month. If you're fortunate enough to invest between $3,000 and $4,000, you'll often find yourself earning a five-figure income weekly with minimal difficulty.

30. ONLINE TUTORING.

You have three options: career tutoring, specialist tutoring, and part-time tutoring. To help you better comprehend your options, here are some extra explanations of your various choices

Voluntary Tutoring.

Students and professionals alike will appreciate the adaptability that these items provide. However, because they are part-time, you must first secure employment with a corporation or internet business and prepare for it. This could be a fantastic option if you are looking for a simple way to earn extra money on the side.

Freelancing is also an option, but it can be tough to handle transactions and negotiations if you are occupied with another endeavor. By getting "hired" online, you can obtain a regular stream of "students" with minimal effort.

Career Tutoring.

With the recent rise in popularity of the online job market, online tutoring jobs are now a viable career option. The beautiful thing about this is that there are numerous ways to accomplish this.

You can either work as a freelancer or establish a firm offering these services. Some may argue that this doesn't qualify as an online tutoring job, but since you will likely begin by teaching the classes yourself, it still allows as such.

Customized Tutoring.

This approach, maybe the most prevalent of the bunch, is available in various formats today. Technically, even one-on-one "coaching" services qualify as specialized tutoring, as you will continue to operate as a "guide" and instruct your customer online.

There are several opportunities to make money online if you have some spare time. You can explore working as an online tutor to assist others with their academic difficulties. Your earnings will determine how well you perform as a tutor and how much time and effort you invest.

The topics requiring the most tutoring are science (chemistry and physics) and math (algebra). It is in such high demand because there is a push for more students to enroll in these subjects. Your expertise in these areas makes online instruction a great option.

The available positions can be found on websites advertising tutoring jobs. On the website, you will find the necessary qualifications and prerequisites. As you navigate the websites, note the application process, which will vary from site to site.

The application will likely include a test and a way to fill it out. Apply to as many internet websites advertising teaching positions as possible, boosting your likelihood of success. You will be evaluated to ensure that your experience is legitimate. They will inform you if your submission was successful.

Your tutoring hours must be determined, as most companies seeking tutors want a minimum number of hours per week. It is a minimal requirement, although it is possible to work more. This is entirely up to you, provided that your schedule permits it. The majority of employers will limit your weekly hours to thirty.

At least once every month, you will get a direct bank payment or a cheque in the mail. It is proportional to the number of hours done. During the application process, the method of compensation is described. You must complete an agreement document before beginning work.

The tutoring agency that employs you will supply you with students. You will also receive the materials essential to assure your success. It ensures compliance with protocols. If you have any questions, ask your tutor agent for clarification.

Having students from various backgrounds and walks of life may make being an online tutor satisfying and exciting. While tutoring, you earn money and experience the excitement of helping another person.

CONCLUSION.

As you may or may not know, starting a business isn't easy. It requires a lot of planning, including local market analysis, a site, some personnel, and a substantial amount of operating equipment.

Not because you did not do your research but because that is the nature of business; all these necessities will result in a substantial expenditure and a great danger of things not happening as planned.

Obviously, the greater the attention to detail and the more comprehensive the planning, the greater the likelihood of success. In any case, a conventional business like that will load you with many expenses that will keep you from earning a single dollar for at least a year.

Therefore, even though entrepreneurship is the way to go, it is possible to develop and operate a profitable business from which you can earn enough money to live comfortably without the stress of having thousands of dollars at risk for months or even years.

So, what is the answer to your entrepreneurial urge if you don't have the capital or don't like to risk too much of it yet wish to earn money quickly?

Start an internet business, which is much more than selling on eBay or Amazon. I know that an eCommerce business can be lucrative. Still, after many years of generating a living online, I prefer more time- and cost-efficient solutions that give better short- and long-term growth potential, starting with relatively minimal inputs.

Internet marketing is a clear example - though not the only one - of this type of opportunity, as it allows you to develop a sustainable business capable of generating thousands of dollars in monthly revenue without risking thousands of dollars.

Internet marketing is certainly more about knowing than investing. Thus, whereas a traditional firm needs 60% capital investment and 40% know-how, an internet marketing-based online business will need 5% capital investment (primarily in educational resources) and 95% know-how.

This means you will be risking time and effort rather than money when you conduct business online through internet marketing or any other method that enables you to conduct your organization online.

This doesn't imply you can afford to be wasteful, though, as your time and effort are equally precious resources (remember, time is money). Even if you have little or no money, you have all it takes to run a great business right now, with the peace of mind that you have nothing to lose other than some of your energy, which is a renewable resource.

Therefore, if you start a business online, you will have room for trial and error without fear of losing a fortune and the distinct advantage that many online business options, such as internet marketing, forex trading, and stock trading offer, which is the ability to deliver actual results within days of having begun, assuming you have the proper tools and resources at your disposal.

Management Skills for Managers.

1. Time Management for Managers
2. Employee Coaching for Managers
3. Team Building for Managers
4. Self Confidence for Managers
5. Negotiation Skills for Managers
6. Customer Service Skills for Managers
7. Assertiveness for Managers
8. Business Etiquette for Managers
9. Listening Skills for Managers
10. Leadership Skills for Managers
11. Communication Skills for Managers
12. Presentation Skills for Managers
13. Stress Management for Managers
14. Decision Making for Managers
15. Conflict Management for Managers.

Series: Financial Freedom at Any Age.

- Achieving Financial Freedom in your 20's
- Achieving Financial Freedom in your 30's
- Achieving Financial Freedom in your 40's
- Achieving Financial Freedom in your 50's
- Achieving Financial Freedom in your 60's
- Achieving Financial Freedom in your 70's and beyond.
- Achieving Financial Freedom in children
- Achieving Financial Freedom in teenagers
- Achieving Financial Freedom in college students.
- Financial Scams to be Aware of in Retirement.

Series: Personal Finance for You.
- ➢ Buying and Selling Crypto for Beginners
- ➢ Why Investing in Dividend Stocks Makes Sense.

Series: Wealth 2022.

- ➢ Online Entrepreneurship.
- ➢ Starting Your Own Business
- ➢ Wealth Management
- ➢ Passive Income.
- ➢ 12 Steps to Starting your own business.

Series: Excellent Customer Service

- ➢ Excellent Customer Service in Retail
- ➢ Excellent Customer Service in Fast Food
- ➢ Excellent Customer Service in Full-Service Restaurant
- ➢ Excellent Customer Service in Teaching.
- ➢ Excellent Customer Service in Real Estate
- ➢ Excellent Customer Service in a Call Center
- ➢ Excellent Customer Service as a Receptionist
- ➢ Excellent Customer Service in a Hotel
- ➢ Excellent Customer Service in Selling
- ➢ Excellent Customer Service No Matter the Situation.

- Excellent Customer Service in Dental Office
- Excellent Customer Service in Medical Office.

Series: Quick Money.

- Quick Money in a Week
- Quick Money in a Weekend
- Quick Money in a Month
- Quick Money for Students.

Series: How to Promote

- How to Make your Business Thrive During a Recession
- How to Promote your Recipe Book
- How to Promote your Children Book.

Author Bio

D.K. Hawkins. D.K. enjoys reading personal business books as well as spending time outdoors. More books will come in this collection, so please follow on Amazon for more books.

Thank you for your purchase of this book.

I honestly do appreciate it and appreciate you, my excellent customer.

God Bless You.

D.K. Hawkins.

www.ingramcontent.com/pod-product-compliance
Lightning Source LLC
Chambersburg PA
CBHW070241220526
45465CB00004B/1483